place of caring and love—for their company, for their organization, for the people who work for them, and for themselves. I encourage you to read the book as part of your own leadership journey; I promise you will learn something new about yourself and expand both your "hard" and "soft" leadership capabilities.

~ Melendy Lovett

I0096586

Shaunna has been an amazing mentor and coach. Her wisdom and heart combined to ask the right questions to help me discover what an integrated life looks like for me, which has purpose, clarity, and well being. She has also provided an extra dose of encouragement when I had to make some tough choices in order to materialize the best path for me.

~ Valerie Mason Davis

Shaunna is a heart-centered mentor and coach who nurtures leadership from a place of empathy and courage—empowering people to shine authentically, build genuine connections, and step into their power with meaning and joy.

~ Gayatri Kesavanmurthy

Shaunna is a heart-centered leadership coach who keeps me performing at my best by actively listening, removing blockages, and offering guidance on each item I bring to our coaching sessions. She is the epitome of a judgement-free leader, which allows me to comfortably discuss any and all items that are in my path. I can say with confidence that I am a different professional, leader, and person because of Shaunna's coaching and mentorship.

~ *Randall Thomas*

In this book, Shaunna captures and shares her proven people and organization leadership model that has enabled her amazing success first as an educator, next as a global senior executive in technology manufacturing, and now as an executive coach in technology, software, manufacturing, and non-profits. What sets the book apart is its focus on the responsibilities that come with stepping into a people-leadership role. Shaunna emphasizes that becoming an excellent people leader is a learning process requiring ongoing internal work, starting with knowing yourself incredibly well. Shaunna takes readers from there to the criticality and process of building relationships, culture, and organizations—all absolute requirements for enduring high-impact people leadership.

Finally, this book fully embraces the idea that, even though few leaders really talk about it, the very best and most effective leaders lead from a

Leading with Heart

A Guide to Mindset, Relationships, and Culture

Shaunna Black

KI Productions

KI PRODUCTIONS
Where every story matters

DEDICATION

To my mother, Peggy, and my father, Bob, who taught me to love, live with purpose, and be a leader who serves others.

CONTENTS

Foreword

I first met Shaunna Black 25 years ago when she was a senior leader at Texas Instruments. At the time, she was sitting on the board of the Texas Women's Foundation, where I was an emerging leader in my early 30s. She impressed me in every meeting with the frank, candid professionalism she brought, coupled with tangible warmth and care for every person in the room, even amid disagreements. It immediately became something that I wanted to emulate. At the time, it didn't have a name —but what Shaunna was living out, even then, was essentially the embodiment of the contents of this book on Heart-Centered Leadership.

When I left the Texas Women's Foundation in 2003 to return to policy research at the RAND Corporation, Shaunna and I lost touch for several years. But when I had my first run-in several years later with challenging leadership dynamics that were beyond my ability to navigate on my own as I moved up, Shaunna was the first person I called to ask if she would coach me through to higher ground. Thankfully, she said yes – and I would say it is because of all that I learned from her coaching and friendship through the years that today people turn to me for similar mentorship, education, and coaching. Heart-centered leadership creates all kinds of virtuous circles, with leaders giving to those that work with them what they most need in a current moment, as well as what their employees need from those leaders down the road as they continue the pass-it-on process of sharing and embodying this special caring + leadership approach that leads to a culture of flourishing and optimal performance.

Shaunna was the first to talk to me about managing my energy as a leader, for my own productivity and the well-being of the team I was managing. She taught me to align my presence with my purpose. And she wrested the old model from me that I had been taught about rigidly making work only about work, showing me instead that getting to deeply know and cultivate relationships with all the people behind the work not only produced better work products, but also higher retention rates, fewer problems requiring HR, and many deep and lasting friendships that have been maintained over decades, even though we no longer work together.

Why is this book needed now? In an age of ongoing return-to-office debates and the emergence and expansion of AI, it is the elements of humanity in the workplace that will ultimately set organizations apart. Do people feel seen and appreciated for their contributions? Do they feel like the feedback meant to grow them into a better version of themselves is given in such a way that they can hear and absorb it, because they can feel the person providing the feedback truly cares about them? If you want as a leader to be a part of actively shaping a culture of safety, connection, productivity, and growth – and are attracted to the idea that it actually can be done through compassion and love – then this book can help get you there.

For those for whom the mention of love in a workplace context initially makes you squirm slightly, read up on what Gallup's research says are the 12 needs that managers can meet to improve their employees' productivity. Four of them are listed here:

> ** My supervisor, or someone at work, seems to care about me as a person.*

* There is someone at work who encourages my development.

* In the last six months, someone at work has talked to me about my progress.

* This last year, I have had opportunities at work to learn and grow.

These questions, when answered affirmatively, have been shown to result in a more productive and engaged workforce. The pages of this book will take you on a journey that leads you to a different land of work and care, teaching you new ways to conceive of and practice your leadership – today and every day.

Finally, as a teaser... one of my personal favorite quotes of this manuscript is the following, given it perfectly encapsulates what we're ultimately going for as leaders:

"Leadership means showing up—not just when things are going well, but when they're falling apart. It means being the person someone can call when they've made a mistake, when they're overwhelmed, or when they need a reminder of their worth.

This isn't about rescuing people. It's about standing with them. It's about holding space, speaking truth, and reminding them who they are. That's leadership."

You've read the foreword. Now take the next step. May it help you as it has helped my teams and me over time – enabled us to become flourishing, thriving, and highly productive teams... that, as colleagues, often become friends as well.

I feel honored to count Shaunna Black among them as a friend.

To your reading journey!

Sarah Cotton Nelson

Founder and Principal, High Flying Strategy

INTRODUCTION

We are living and leading in a world that is changing faster than ever—technology is advancing, globalization is reshaping economies, and social norms are being rewritten in real time. Amid this complexity, people are searching for anchors they can trust. They're not just seeking competent and creative leaders. They're seeking courageous leaders who invite differing perspectives and encourage learning and growth.

Throughout my leadership journey, spanning education, corporate technology, nonprofit service, and coaching, I've observed what works and what breaks people down. Too often, I worked under transactional, top-down management styles that kept people in a state of survival. I was also blessed with heart-centered leaders who changed everything with one simple commitment: they led with love.

Those leaders taught me what I now know to be true: leadership is personal. It's relational. It starts from within.

Leading with Heart was born from years of leading global teams, mentoring emerging leaders, navigating cultural transformation, and doing the inner work of becoming the kind of person I would want to follow. It's also rooted in a deep belief that every person is uniquely made—and uniquely called—to lead in their own way.

This guide is not a "how-to" manual. It's a reflection guide. It's an invitation. A quiet, powerful return to what matters most: who we are, how we treat people, and the kind of environments we build every day—by design or by default.

If you're leading a team, coaching leaders, mentoring, or simply trying to show up more authentically in your work, I wrote this book for you.

The book is organized into five movements:

- Who Am I? — Leadership begins with self-awareness and wholeness.

- How Do I Show Up? — Purpose and authenticity create trust.

- Who Are We Together? — Relationships are built one person at a time.

- What Are We Building? — Culture is shaped by everyday choices.

- Love at the Center — Love is the energy driving the sustainable momentum of your organization.

You won't find quick fixes here. But you will find reflection, encouragement, and simple truths when leadership feels messy, hard, or lonely.

My hope is that with this book, you find someone who believes in you - someone who reminds you that your heart is not a liability. It is your greatest asset.

—Shaunna

CHAPTER 1

WHO AM I?

"Knowing yourself is the beginning of all wisdom." —*Aristotle*

What makes you, you? Even when people share the same home, the same table, and the same experiences, we emerge uniquely ourselves.

At our kitchen table, my brother was the jokester, my sister the listener, and I was the planner. Same parents. Same schools. Same relocations. Yet today, we've built remarkably different lives. Our parenting styles, careers, priorities, and even the way we rest and restore look different.

While we shared a home, we were never the same people. We were always uniquely made.

I believe we all are.

Each of us is a one-of-a-kind creation. Our personality, our energy, our story, our joy, our pain—it's all part of our design. We are not meant to lead like anyone else. The most powerful leadership begins when we stop trying to imitate others and learn to lead as ourselves.

There's a freedom that comes when you no longer feel the pressure to perform or conform. I'd rather be a first-class Shaunna than a second-class version of someone else. It took me years to understand that. At times, I tried to fit into environments where my natural style felt too soft, too relational, or too "different." Yet the truth is this: my ability to connect deeply, to care about the person in front of me, to lead with love—that's my superpower. That's how I lead best.

Listening to the Voice Within

Inside each of us, there's a voice. I call it God or the Divine. Some people call it intuition. Others call it Spirit, the Universe, or Inner Wisdom. It's the voice that knows who we are and reminds us who we're becoming. That voice doesn't shout. It isn't demanding. It invites. It whispers truth when we get quiet enough to listen.

When we learn to listen to that inner voice, we stop leading from a place of striving and start leading from a place of guidance. We begin to live and lead from the inside out.

The challenge is that we also have another voice —the voice of the ego. This voice is afraid, protective, reactive, and addicted to comparison. It wants to be liked, accepted, and rewarded.

The ego isn't the enemy; it's a part of us, shaped by our experiences, our pain, and the stories we've been told. If we let the ego lead, we end up performing rather than showing up authentically.

That's why self-awareness is essential.

The best leaders I know are deeply self-aware. They understand their own patterns, triggers, and blind spots. They've done the work to integrate their stories. They know their core values. They know when they're leading from love and when fear has slipped into the driver's seat.

Making the Unconscious Conscious

Carl Jung once said, "Until you make the unconscious conscious, it will direct your life and you will call it fate." That truth shaped how I saw leadership—and myself. Practices that reveal my unconscious beliefs and motivations have become a daily routine. These practices have helped me gain a better understanding of myself. Being a conscious leader is important to me.

So much of how we lead is shaped by what we've buried: the messages we internalized as children, the beliefs we formed during difficult times, and the habits we adopted to survive. If we don't examine those things, we will repeat them—and we'll pass them on through the families and cultures we create.

For me, practices such as prayer, journaling, reflection, and seeking feedback from trusted advisors have become part of my daily rhythm. These practices help me notice what I'm carrying and whether fear or love is leading. They remind me that becoming a conscious leader is a daily choice.

Leadership doesn't start with a mission statement. It starts with the question: What's going on inside of me?

- Am I divinely led or ego-driven?

- Am I leading from my wisdom or my wounds?

- Am I showing up with purpose or performing for approval?

- Am I value-driven or trying to avoid failure?

These are not just personal questions. They are leadership questions. Everything unresolved in us will eventually show up in how we lead others.

Your Energy Matters

Have you ever walked into a room and immediately felt the tension—or the warmth? That's energy. Our energy is contagious.

Our emotional state as leaders affects everyone around us. If we're stressed, rushed, defensive, or detached, our people will feel it. If we're grounded, curious, honest, and open-hearted, they'll feel that too. We don't always realize it, but our energy introduces us before we speak a word.

I remember walking into a meeting one morning after carrying stress from an earlier conversation. I hadn't said a word, but within minutes the team had gone quiet and guarded.

Later, one person told me, "It felt like you were upset with us before we even started." My energy had spoken for me. That experience reminded me that the way I enter a space is just as important as what I communicate within it.

Self-leadership means managing that energy with care. It means paying attention to what drains us and what fuels us. It means noticing when we're reactive and learning to pause instead of powering through. It means asking for help, setting boundaries, resting when needed, and telling the truth—especially to ourselves.

When we're aware of how we're showing up, we can choose to shift. We can lead with intention rather than instinct.

When this happens consistently, something incredible unfolds: our presence becomes a source of safety and inspiration for others. We become leaders people trust—not because we're perfect, but because we're real.

The Power of Knowing Yourself

The first step to becoming a heart-centered leader isn't reading another book or mastering a new strategy. It's slowing down long enough to get to know yourself.

You are not too much. You are not too soft. You are not inadequate. You are here, on purpose, with a gift that only you can offer the world. The more you accept and honor who you are, the more powerful your leadership becomes.

This work—this worthwhile, lifelong work of knowing and growing yourself—is the foundation of every great team, every healthy culture, and every meaningful legacy. When you know who you are, you stop leading from fear. When fear no longer drives you, the people around you begin to flourish.

That's where leadership begins—inside you, rooted in self-awareness, ready to ripple outward.

Leadership Truth

Self-awareness isn't self-indulgent—it's the foundation of all authentic leadership.

Reflection Prompts

What part of my inner world—a value, belief, or voice—have I been ignoring or undervaluing?

How might honoring it change the way I lead?

"True influence and effective leadership aren't found in constant outward action, but in a profound internal journey: reflection... the silent mirror revealing our true selves and guiding our path."

— *Khandelwal, A. K.*

CHAPTER 2

How Do I Show Up?

*"Honesty and transparency make you
vulnerable. Be honest and
transparent anyway."*
—Mother Theresa

Leadership isn't just about what we do. It's
about who we are and how we show up. When
people experience us, they don't just remember
the words we said or the tasks we completed—
they remember the energy, presence, and
authenticity we carried into the room.

Our presence is often louder than our position.
It can inspire trust and confidence, or it can
create distance and doubt.

Early in my leadership journey, I thought
showing up meant projecting strength at all
costs. I believed I had to have the answers, mask
my struggles, and push forward no matter

what. But over time, I discovered that presence isn't about perfection—it's about authenticity. People don't need us to be flawless; they need us to be real.

The Mirror We Hold

How we show up often reflects what's happening inside of us. If we're hurried, distracted, or fearful, that energy spills out onto the people around us. If we're grounded, attentive, and hopeful, people sense it. Our teams become mirrors of our presence.

This doesn't mean we'll never have hard days. It means being aware of how those days affect the people we lead. Sometimes the most powerful thing we can do is pause, acknowledge what we're carrying, and choose how we want to enter the room.

A mentor once told me: "Your presence is your leadership." That truth has guided me again and again. It reminds me that showing up with intention is often more important than showing up with a perfect plan.

The Courage of Authenticity

Showing up authentically requires courage. It asks us to bring our whole selves—the strengths and the struggles. It means owning our mistakes instead of hiding them, asking for help instead of pretending we don't need it, and admitting when we don't have the answer.

Authenticity creates trust. When people see us leading with honesty and transparency rather than armor they feel permission to do the same. They show up more authentically themselves. That's how strong teams are built—not with masks, but being ourselves.

Authenticity also invites connection. When we share the "why" behind our decisions, when we let people see our values in action, when we express gratitude sincerely, we show people that we value them.

Lead With Purpose

Every time we walk into a room, we bring something with us. The question is: does our presence align with our purpose?

If we want to build trust, are we showing up in ways that invite openness?

If we want to encourage growth, are we creating space for questions and learning?

If we want to lead with love, are we slowing down long enough to connect with the people present?

Alignment doesn't happen by accident. It happens when we know who we are (Chapter 1) and choose to show up authentically. It happens when we ground ourselves before difficult conversations, when we listen more than we speak, and when we model our values.

Practices That Shape Our Presence

Small but powerful practices can elevate the way we show up:

- Pause before entering. Take a breath, set an intention, and decide what energy you want to bring into the room.

- Listen fully. Give people the gift of your full attention.

- Check your alignment. Match your tone, body language and presence to your purpose and values.

- Be honest and human. If you're having a hard day, acknowledge it without projecting it.

- Let people see your vulnerability.

These practices remind us that showing up is not about performing—it's about being present with purpose.

The Ripple Effect

The way we show up doesn't end with us. It ripples outward. Our energy can either calm or escalate a tense situation. Our presence can either spark creativity or shut it down. Our behavior can either encourage others or keep them guarded.

When we show up with purpose, presence, and authenticity, we create a space where others can do the same. That's the kind of leadership that multiplies talent—not by control, but by influence.

Leadership Truth

Your presence and authenticity is your leadership. How you show up shapes how others experience you.

Reflection Prompts

When I walk into a room, what do people feel before I even speak?

How can I better align my presence and authenticity with my purpose?

"Authenticity is a collection of choices that we have to make every day. It's about the choice to show up and be real. The choice to be honest. The choice to let our true selves be seen."

—Brené Brown

CHAPTER 3

WHO ARE WE TOGETHER?

"The test of leadership is not to put greatness into humanity, but to elicit it, for the greatness is already there." —James Buchanan

The most impactful seasons of my life aren't defined by achievements, promotions, or metrics. They're defined by people.

I remember the mentors who believed in me before I believed in myself. The colleagues who showed up with kindness when I was struggling. The teams that became community —not because we were perfect, but because we chose to trust one another and make commitments to each other.

Those relationships made me braver, wiser, and more human. They also made me a better leader.

Leadership is not about control or authority. It's about connection. It's about creating relationships where people feel seen, growth can happen, and mistakes can become lessons that strengthen us. It's about building a container—a space—that's strong enough to hold both truth and grace.

Everything we do as leaders happens inside the space of a relationship. The quality of that relationship shapes everything that flows from it.

The Container of Relationships

Think of a glass jar. If it's strong, clear, and well cared for, you can fill it with something precious and trust that it will hold. If it's cracked, brittle, or neglected, whatever's poured in won't be safe.

Relationships work the same way.

When the relationship between a leader and a team member is strong—built on trust, mutual respect, and honest communication—amazing things happen. Feedback becomes easier. Creativity flows. Accountability is embraced instead of feared.

When the relationship is weak or broken, even well-intentioned feedback can land as judgment. Even celebration can feel performative. Safety disappears.

When the container is fragile, even good intentions spill out and are lost. But when the container is strong, it can hold not just success, but also struggle, disappointment, and repair. That's the real test of relationship: not whether it works when things are going well, but whether it holds when things get hard.

Our Shared Humanity

Our relationships—especially those we form as leaders—are sanctified spaces. They are spaces where connections are intentional, respectful, and nurtured. Here, trust deepens, growth happens, and people feel safe to share their full humanity. In this space, leaders see both the preciousness of the human and our shared humanity as part of the divine whole. We support and bear witness to our journey together.

We lead people with dreams, families, responsibilities, gifts, and histories. When we remember this, we lead differently. We slow down. We listen more closely. We become curious instead of critical. We communicate from the heart, not just from the head.

This is how we create a culture of belonging.

People will forgive mistakes in strategy. They will forgive reorganization. They will forgive the occasional oversight or miscommunication. What they won't forget is how we made them feel. Did they feel safe? Did they feel seen? Did they feel like they mattered?

That is what remains.

Creating Culture, One Relationship at a Time

We often think of "culture" as something organizational—a big concept managed by HR or shaped by company values on the wall. The truth is, culture is created moment by moment, in the spaces between people.

Every relationship you cultivate as a leader becomes a microcosm of the culture you're building. If you're building trust one person at a time, showing up with honesty, and leading with compassion—you are actively shaping a culture of safety, connection, and potential. If you show up blameful and critical, you are actively shaping a culture of fear and self-protection. Potential is wasted.

Your influence is undeniable. Are you creating the culture you want?

High Trust, High Growth

I've had the privilege of working inside high-trust environments—and I've also experienced environments where trust was an afterthought. The difference is palpable.

Trust is deeply personal and grows over time. Trust grows:

- When people can count on us to do what we say we'll do

- When we own our mistakes

- When we show what they share with us, it stays with us

- When we follow through on our commitments

- When we're courageous, instead of playing it safe

Trust is not a vague concept. It's deeply personal. It grows when we tell the truth— even when it's hard. It grows when we see humanity in one another, not just productivity. In high-trust teams, people don't waste energy protecting themselves. They spend that energy creating. They're not performing; they're contributing. They're not trying to survive the culture; they're helping shape it.

That kind of trust creates the conditions for growth. Growth, after all, is the goal—not only organizational growth, but human growth.

When we see people not as replaceable resources but as unique, gifted, complex humans, we naturally want to serve their growth. We ask better questions, give meaningful feedback, and create environments where they can experiment, stretch, and thrive.

High trust isn't easy. It requires courage to build spaces where people can be honest, try new things, and come as they are—without fear. It means aligning our purpose, being clear about our goals, and succeeding together.

Trust doesn't erase challenges, but it changes how we face them. A team with trust can walk into the unknown with curiosity instead of fear. A team without it will shrink back and protect themselves. You set the tone as a leader.

Authority Versus Vulnerability

From a young age, most of us are taught to respect authority—parents, teachers, coaches, leaders. In organizations, that authority is amplified through titles, roles, and responsibilities. Leaders carry the power to hire or fire, assign projects, promote, reward—or withhold. That power can easily create barriers in relationships.

I remember early in my career feeling the weight of positional power. My title gave me authority, but it didn't automatically earn me trust. Trust came only when I stepped out from behind the title and chose to show up as a person first.

Heart-centered leadership calls us to use this power with our people, not over them. Our purpose is to build nurturing teams and organizations where we succeed together. Healthy relationships are the building blocks of that success.

Vulnerability is the antidote to positional power. Building trust with the people we lead begins with us. We must step out from behind the armor of authority. We must create safety so we can connect as people.

That means investing time and energy in respectful, warm relationships, valuing each other's stories, and supporting each other's needs. Every interaction becomes a moment of trust and relationship-building.

The Power of Empathy

Empathy supercharges trust and psychological safety. As Daniel Pink said, "Empathy is about standing in someone else's shoes, feeling with his or her heart, seeing with his or her eyes."

Relationships grow when people feel seen, heard, and understood. Empathy helps people feel: I belong here. My leader cares about me.

I once had a team member who carried herself with confidence but rarely asked for help. At first, I assumed she didn't need support. Instead of pressing, I slowed down, asked questions, and listened. Over time, she shared that she feared being seen as weak. By practicing empathy instead of judgment, I was able to offer flexibility and encouragement—and in turn, her trust and engagement grew.

Empathy is not abstract; it's practiced in simple, human ways:

- Seeking to understand another's perspective

- Being willing to feel with them

- Taking action to help

When empathy and trust are present, leaders create alignment around a shared purpose and influence without coercion or fear. Conflict is reduced. Creativity expands. People bring their best because they feel safe to do so.

Coaching Accountability

Personal responsibility and accountability are learned skills. They're linked to confidence— the belief that we can create the outcomes we desire. As Bob Proctor once said, "Accountability is the glue that ties commitment to results."

People show accountability in different ways, usually shaped by their life experiences and what they saw modeled. Those with high accountability see problems as opportunities. They make a plan, take action, and keep adjusting until they get the result they want. Others may struggle more with accountability. Sometimes they don't see the problem or they shift blame instead of owning their part. Others might understand the issues but still hope for someone else to step in and fix it for them.

As leaders, our role is not to rescue but to empower. Helping someone grow in accountability is not about shaming them—it's about believing in their capabilities. When we hold people accountable, we call out their strength. We give them the dignity of discovering their own resilience.

We can help people grow by asking thoughtful questions:

- What have you tried?

- What's an easy next step?

- What else could you do?

- What have you done in the past to solve this kind of problem?

- Who could help?

- What might remove that barrier?

- How can I support you?

We communicate our belief in their capability. We act as thought partners. We encourage and guide as needed, but ultimately allow them to discover that they are capable of delivering the outcomes they want. That discovery is one of the greatest gifts we can give.

Sitting in the Mess Together

A friend once described trust as "the willingness to sit in the mess with someone." That image has never left me.

Leadership means showing up—not just when things are going well, but when they're falling apart. It means being the person someone can call when they've made a mistake, when they're overwhelmed, or when they simply need to be reminded of their worth.

This isn't about rescuing people. It's about standing with them. Holding space. Speaking truth. Reminding them who they are. That's leadership.

When we do this consistently, we don't just build loyalty—we build transformation. We create relationships that ripple outward, shaping culture, influencing families, and even changing communities. The way we lead together becomes the story we leave behind.

Leadership Truth

The quality of our leadership is shaped by the quality of our relationships.

Reflection Prompts

In my closest relationships—at work or home— where am I strengthening our connection?

Where might I need to deepen or repair a relationship?

"Trust is the highest form of human motivation. It brings out the very best in people."

—*Stephen R. Covey*

CHAPTER 4

WHAT ARE WE BUILDING?

"The greatest leaders mobilize others by coalescing people around a shared vision [purpose]."
—Ken Blanchard

One of the greatest truths I've learned as a leader is this: culture is not a byproduct—it is a design. Culture is shaped in every meeting, every hallway conversation, every performance review, and every decision we make about what gets celebrated, tolerated, or ignored. It is the invisible architecture that holds—or hinders—everything we try to build.

Yet in many organizations, culture is treated as an afterthought. It's something people hope will "just happen" if the right people are hired or the right slogans are written. Culture doesn't work that way. If we want to build something that lasts—something that helps people thrive—we have to design it on purpose. I've walked into workplaces where the culture was magnetic. You could feel the energy, the clarity, and the shared sense of belonging the moment you stepped through the door. I've also walked into places where it felt like everyone was holding their breath, where innovation was stifled, and where people kept their heads down to survive.

The difference wasn't the industry or the talent pool.

The difference was leadership.

Culture Begins With Purpose

As leaders, we are architects of the environment. That doesn't mean we control everything, but it does mean we are responsible for the container. That responsibility begins with clarity of purpose. Purpose is what pulls people forward. It aligns vision with action. It gives meaning to the work.

When people know why their work matters, they begin to care deeply about how they do it. Purpose doesn't live in a binder on a shelf. It lives in our decisions, our behaviors, and our energy. It doesn't even have to start at the top of the organization. It can begin right where you are as a leader. You are the culture leader for your team - NOT just the managers above you.

In one of my most fulfilling leadership roles, our department wasn't just focused on outcomes—we were aligned around a shared purpose: to serve others, to grow together, and to create a place where people could become their best selves. That clarity infused everything. It made hard conversations worth having. It made collaboration easier. It gave meaning to our commitments to our coworkers and business partners.

I've also seen what happens when purpose is unclear. In one organization, people worked hard, but without shared meaning, the work felt heavy. Meetings were filled with confusion. Burnout spread quickly because no one knew what the "why" was behind the "what." Once leaders reconnected the team to its deeper purpose, energy returned and collaboration flourished. Purpose doesn't make the work easy. It makes it worth it.

People Don't Fit Into Culture—They Shape It

Too often, we treat people as interchangeable parts in a machine—easily replaced, managed by process, judged by numbers. But people aren't parts. They are the heart and soul of the organization.

I've seen organizations preach values like innovation and teamwork, while their unspoken expectations communicated a culture of perfectionism and competition. People always read the unspoken rules. You can feel them in the energy of the room, in what's rewarded, in who's promoted, in how feedback is handled, and whether or not it feels safe to speak up. When the stated values and the lived values align, people thrive. When they don't, people protect themselves.

One of the best teams I ever worked with had a leader named Jim, a retired Air Force colonel who embodied the principles of servant leadership. From day one, the message was clear: "We care about people. We work hard, but we have fun. We build trust, and we leave room for life."

You could feel it in the interviews, the meetings, the hallway conversations. Servant leadership wasn't a line on a values chart—it was how we treated each other. It was the lens through which we made every decision.

By contrast, I've also been part of teams where the posters on the wall promised collaboration,

LEADING WITH HEART

but the lived reality was competition. People were careful with their words. Leaders spoke about values in quarterly meetings but behaved in ways that elicited fear. In those environments, people didn't give their best—they did what was safe.

Culture isn't just about what's written down. It's about what's lived.

Designing With Intention

If you're a leader, you're a culture designer—whether you realize it or not. Regardless of the larger organizational climate, you are the culture designer for your team.

You are consistently modeling something: how to treat others, how to handle failure, how to celebrate success, how to listen (or not), and how to deliver on commitments.

The question is: are you designing your leadership environment on purpose, or are you repeating unconscious patterns that undermine your purpose?

Here's what I've learned:

- You don't need a fancy framework to start.

- You need clarity.

37

- You need consistency.

- You need courage to create something different.

Culture change begins with micro-shifts, not sweeping overhauls. It starts when you invite your team to co-create a set of agreements. It starts when you share your leadership philosophy. It starts when you model transparency, even when it's uncomfortable.

In one team I led, a small shift—beginning each meeting with gratitude—changed everything. At first it felt awkward. But over time, the room softened. People looked each other in the eye. They noticed strengths they had overlooked before. That small practice didn't just change our meetings—it changed our relationships.

What we tolerate becomes our culture. What we affirm becomes our legacy.

Creating the Conditions for Growth

Heart-centered leadership doesn't mean avoiding hard conversations. It means leading with care and clarity.

It means creating spaces where feedback is constructive, where roles are respected, where values aren't negotiable, and where every person knows their voice matters.

We empower people when we:

- Align purpose with daily work

- Clarify expectations without micromanaging

- Give stretch opportunities with support

- Help remove barriers within the system

- Coach people to become their best selves

- Celebrate small wins

Feedback is one of the most powerful tools we have for growth—but it can also be one of the most dangerous if mishandled. Feedback that respects, encourages, and calls out potential helps people rise. Feedback that shames shuts people down. Leaders set the tone for which kind it will be.

When we take empowering actions, we stop managing only performance and begin developing people. That's the kind of culture I want to build: one where people aren't just surviving the workweek but growing, contributing, and thriving in it.

You Don't Need Permission to Start

It takes courage, but you don't have to wait for a title, a budget, or an executive sponsor to begin shaping culture. You can start right now in your own circle of influence—your team, your department, your classroom, your office.

Ask yourself:

- What kind of space am I creating for others?

- How do people feel when they leave a meeting with me?

- What messages am I sending through my tone, timing, and attention?

When you lead with intention, the culture around you begins to shift. Maybe not all at once, but steadily, consistently, and powerfully.

You are always building something. Brick by brick. Choice by choice. Let it be something that lasts.

Leadership Truth

Great culture doesn't happen by accident. It happens when leaders choose to care, see and build.

Reflection Prompts

What's one small cultural choice I'm making daily—even unintentionally—that's shaping my team or organization?

Does it reflect who I really want us to be?

"Management is about arranging and telling. Leadership is about nurturing and enhancing."

—*Tom Peters*

CHAPTER 5

LOVE AT THE CENTER

"Love is one of the most powerful yet undervalued virtues a leader can practice."
— *John Mackey*
(co-founder of Whole Foods)

Love isn't a word we use often in corporate spaces. It's been labeled too soft, too emotional, too messy. Yet love is the fiercest, most transformative force a leader can use.

When I talk about heart-centered leadership, I'm not talking about sentimentality. I'm talking about the kind of love that sees the depth in people. The kind of love that believes in someone's potential, even when they can't see it themselves. The kind of love that calls people higher—not by force, but by invitation.

Love is what makes leadership personal. Without it, we're just managing tasks. With it, we're shaping lives.

Love as a Leadership Strategy

Somewhere along the way, we separated love from leadership. We started measuring success only by outcomes—revenue, profit, customer satisfaction or reduced costs—and forgot that people create outcomes. We forgot that belonging and psychological safety aren't just nice-to-haves. They are prerequisites for trust, creativity, and high performance.

I've worked for leaders who led with love and leaders who led with fear. The difference wasn't in their intelligence or skill set. It was in their values. The leaders who shaped me—the ones I still remember—weren't always the most polished or strategic. But they cared. They asked about my family. They noticed when I was quiet. They offered grace when I failed and challenged me to rise when I was ready. They loved their people, and because of that, people chose to follow them.

I've also worked in environments where fear was the primary motivator. Deadlines loomed like weapons. Meetings were charged with tension. People withheld ideas because it felt safer to be silent than to be honest. In those cultures, creativity shriveled, and trust disappeared. The absence of love didn't just damage morale—it diminished performance and wasted potential.

Love builds loyalty. It invites courage. It creates a connection. It unleashes potential, creativity, and commitment. Outstanding growth in revenue, profitability and market share are critical performance outcomes, but they are the byproducts of a culture where people are loved.

The Power of Love

There's a kind of strength in love that the world doesn't always recognize. It's not loud. It doesn't need a title. It's not performative. Yet it's powerful.

Love shows up in the courage to tell the truth with kindness.

It shows up in staying present when someone is struggling.

It shows up in believing the best when trust is shaken.

It shows up in forgiveness, in coaching, and in honoring the dignity of others.

It shows up in growth, success and celebration.

I've been told that love makes leadership weak. I've found the opposite to be true. The strongest leaders I've ever known were also the most loving.

They didn't control others—they didn't need to. Their purpose, presence and power to elevate everyone created such trust and safety that people naturally rose to meet the moment. People got stronger, became accountable, contributed their best, and excelled together.

I think about a difficult performance conversation I once had with a team member. It would have been easy to focus only on mistakes, but instead I began with care: "I see so much potential in you, and I want you to step into it." That conversation, rooted in love and truth, didn't break trust—it strengthened it. She left motivated, not criticized. That's what love does.

Love doesn't remove accountability. It strengthens it. When people know they are valued, they are more willing to commit, grow, and contribute.

Belonging

At the heart of every thriving team is a sense of belonging. Belonging feels like: "You are wanted here. You fit here. You are valued here."

The difference is profound.

Belonging is the feeling that I can bring all of me—not just the polished parts, but my questions, story, and imperfections. Belonging doesn't erase differences; it honors them. It weaves them into the fabric of the team as strengths, not liabilities.

Love helps us build that kind of culture. It's in the way we honor different perspectives. In how we approach conflict with humility. In how we personalize appreciation. In how we remind each person that they are not just a role —they are a human being worthy of care.

That kind of culture doesn't appear overnight. It's built day by day, relationship by relationship, choice by choice. Once it takes root, though, it's contagious. People who feel loved, valued, and empowered begin to lead others the same way. That's how transformation accelerates.

When organizations cultivate belonging, they don't just retain talent—they unleash it. People bring more of their creativity, energy, and discretionary effort. They want to be here, and they want others to join them.

Letting Love Lead

If you want to lead with love, start by asking:

- What does love ask of me right now?

- How can I lead with both truth and empathy?

- Where can I extend grace without compromising growth?

- What would it look like to lead as if people were sacred?

- Do I believe love can unleash limitless potential?

This is not about perfection. It's about intention. It's about choosing to lead from your wholeness, not your wounds. From wisdom, not fear.

From purpose, not pressure.

When you let love guide your leadership, you become more than a manager of outcomes.

You become a builder of people, a restorer of dignity, and a cultivator of thriving communities.

That is the power of heart-centered leadership.

That is the legacy of love.

Leadership Truth

When we lead with love, we unlock potential—
in others and in ourselves.

Reflection Prompts

*Where am I being called to lead with more love,
purpose, trust, accountability, or grace?*

How can I show up leading powerfully with love?

———

Love at the center is more than a leadership
principle—it's a way of life. When we choose
to lead with love, every chapter of leadership
comes together: knowing ourselves, showing
up with intention, building relationships,
creating communities. Love holds it all. It is
both the foundation and the fruit of heart-
centered leadership.

As you carry these truths forward, remember:
this work doesn't end with the last page. It
begins again every morning, in every
conversation, in every choice to see people as
unique, beloved humans. This is how legacies
are built—by heart-centered leaders who love

first, lead with purpose, and stay deeply committed to the success of both the organization and its people, leaving behind lasting growth and sustainable transformation.

"Leadership is not about being in charge. It is about taking care of those in your charge."

— Simon Sinek

AFTERWORD

Dear Leader,

Thank you for taking the time to journey through these pages. I hope you've felt seen, affirmed, and gently challenged along the way.

This work we do—learning to lead from the inside out—is the journey of a heart-centered leader transforming lives. It isn't always easy, but it is always worth it. Every time you choose purpose over performance, connection over control, and love over fear, you shift the world around you.

Leadership is not a destination we arrive at. It is a way of living—moment by moment, relationship by relationship, decision by decision.

If these words have sparked something in you —an affirmation, a question, a quiet knowing

—trust that. That is the voice within you. That is the beginning of your next chapter.

Let your leadership be rooted in love. Let your relationships be shaped by trust. Let your culture be built with intention. Let your journey begin from the inside out.

You don't need permission to lead with heart. You don't need a title to shape culture. You don't have to wait for all of your resistance to disappear to step into the leader you already are.

Just begin. Start by listening to your own voice. Start by showing up with intention in one relationship. Start by planting one seed of trust in your workplace, your home, or your circle. That is how transformation begins—quietly, courageously, with you.

When you're ready for the next step, I'll be here. Leader of Hearts, the full-length book, will walk with you deeper into this journey. But for now, remember this:

You are already leading. You are already enough —and your heart is more than qualified.

From my heart to yours with deep belief in you,

Shaunna

"Good leaders build products. Great leaders
build cultures. Good leaders deliver results.
Great leaders develop people. Good leaders have
vision. Great leaders have values. Good leaders
are role models at work. Great leaders are role
models in life."

—Adam Grant

Coming Soon

Leader of Hearts

If *Leading with Heart* offered you clarity, grounding, and a renewed sense of purpose in how you show up as a leader, you are going to love what comes next.

Leader of Hearts is Shaunna Black's full-length exploration of heart-centered leadership — a transformative, deeply human approach to leading that goes far beyond the foundations introduced in this book.

While *Leading with Heart* gives you the core principles—mindset, relationships, culture, and love—*Leader of Hearts* takes you deeper.

It expands the journey with:

- Rich stories from real leaders and global teams

- Practical frameworks for shaping

culture, coaching effectively, and navigating conflict

• Deep reflection practices and guided exercises

• Tools for sustaining healthy leadership over time

• A full "Leader of Hearts" model you can apply in any environment—corporate, education, nonprofit, ministry, or home

This guide was designed as your starting point—a thought-provoking, quiet companion to help you return to what matters most in leadership: who you are and how you treat people.

Leader of Hearts is the next chapter.

It will walk with you through the full journey of becoming a leader whose presence builds trust, shapes culture, and transforms the lives around you.

If you're ready to go deeper—into purpose, into wholeness, into leadership that lasts—your next step is coming soon.

About the Author

President, Shaunna Black and Associates

Committed to unleashing human potential, as a heart-centered executive coach, speaker, author, and award-winning tech leader, Shaunna Black helps high-performing leaders and executives navigate complex challenges and transformational moments in their careers.

Whether it's a critical leadership transition, a restructuring, an underperforming business unit, or stepping into a new role without a roadmap, she provides clarity, strategy, and heart-centered guidance to help her clients; smart, capable, and ambitious leaders, leading courageously to achieve extraordinary results.

With over two decades of leadership experience across global technology, industrial manufacturing, and operations in 25+ countries, Shaunna brings a 360-degree perspective as a former Fortune 500 executive, venture operating partner, and management consultant.

Over her career, Shaunna has led complex M&A integrations, scaled global operations, turned around underperforming divisions, and guided organizations through crises such as the 2011 Japan tsunami and global pandemic disruptions. Her work has been recognized with multiple awards, including induction into the Women in Technology International Hall of Fame.

Through executive coaching, Shaunna guides leaders to unlock their full potential, navigate complex challenges with confidence, and inspire transformation within themselves and their organizations. Her approach is rooted in heart-centered leadership, a dedication to serving others, and the conviction that when leaders succeed, the people and organizations around them thrive.

www.ingramcontent.com/pod-product-compliance
Lightning Source LLC
Chambersburg PA
CBHW052025030426
42335CB00026B/3287